Holidays and Festivals

A World of Festivals

Rebecca Rissman

www.heinemannraintree.com
Visit our website to find out
more information about
Heinemann-Raintree books.

To order:

☎ Phone 888-454-2279

💻 Visit www.heinemannraintree.com
to browse our catalog and order online.

© 2013 Heinemann Library
an imprint of Capstone Global Library, LLC
Chicago, Illinois

Customer Service: 888-454-2279
Visit our website at www.heinemannraintree.com

All rights reserved. No part of this publication may be reproduced or
transmitted in any form or by any means, electronic or mechanical,
including photocopying, recording, taping, or any information storage
and retrieval system, without permission in writing from the publisher.

Edited by Rebecca Rissman, Daniel Nunn, and Harriet Milles
Designed by Joanna Hinton-Malivoire
Picture research by Elizabeth Alexander
Originated by Capstone Global Library Ltd.
Production by Victoria Fitzgerald
Printed and bound in China by Leo Paper Products Ltd

15 14 13
10 9 8 7 6 5 4 3 2

Library of Congress Cataloging-in-Publication Data
Rissman, Rebecca.
  A world of festivals / Rebecca Rissman.
      p. cm.
  Includes bibliographical references and index.
  ISBN 978-1-4329-5354-6 (hc)—ISBN 978-1-4329-5499-4 (pb) 1.
Festivals. 2. Holidays. I. Title.
  GT3930.R56 2012
  394.26—dc22   2010044798

Acknowledgments
The author and publishers are grateful to the following for permission
to reproduce copyright material: Alamy **p.11 left** (© Blend Images);
Corbis **pp. 8** (© JLP/Jose L. Pelaez), **16** (© T. Mughal/epa); Getty
Images **pp. 6** (Leland Bobbe/Stone), **10** (AFP), **17 left** (Jaafar
Ashtiyeh/AFP), **17 right** (Asif Hassan/AFP), **18** (Yellow Dog
Productions), **19 right** (altrendo images); iStockphoto **p. 21** (©
Matt Olsen); Photolibrary **pp. 5 left** (Vidler Vidler), **7** (Demotix),
12 (Hemant Mehta/India Picture), **15 left** (James and James
Photography/Brand X Pictures); Shutterstock **pp. 4** (© michael
rubin), **5 right** (© Racheal Grazias), **9** (© Jose Gil), **11 right** (©
Hannes Eichinger), **13 left** (© Mahantesh C Morabad), **13 right**
(© gmwnz), **14, 15 right** (© Golden Pixels LLC), **20 left & right**
(© Monkey Business Images), **19 left** (© haak78), **21** (© Monkey
Business Images), **22** (© Christophe Testi).

Front cover photograph of people watching a fireworks display
reproduced with permission of Corbis (© Firefly Productions).
Back cover photograph of Chinese children performing
reproduced with permission of Shutterstock (© Christophe Testi).

Every effort has been made to contact copyright holders of any
material reproduced in this book. Any omissions will be rectified in
subsequent printings if notice is given to the publisher.

Some words appear in bold, **like this.** You can find out
what they mean in "Words to Know" on page 23.

Contents

About this series

Books in this series introduce readers to different special days celebrated around the world. Use this book to stimulate discussion about how people recognize religious and secular holidays throughout the year.

Holidays and Festivals

People celebrate holidays and festivals all around the world. Holidays and festivals are special days. People spend time together and have fun.

Different people celebrate different holidays and festivals. But all holidays and festivals are special.

Some holidays and festivals are part of a **religion** or belief. People who share the same religion gather together to take part in these celebrations.

Some holidays and festivals celebrate a special person who did something good. Other holidays celebrate a country.

New Year's Day

People around the world celebrate the New Year in different ways. The New Year is the start of a new **calendar**. Some people celebrate the New Year on the 1st of January.

Some people celebrate the New Year on different days. Chinese people celebrate New Year on a different day each year. To celebrate the Chinese New Year, people watch **parades** and give gifts.

Easter

Christian people celebrate Easter all around the world. Many Christian people go to church on Easter Day. Easter happens in March or April each year.

Easter egg

People celebrate Easter in different ways. On Easter morning, some people hunt for Easter eggs. Some people bake special cakes. Some people eat special food.

Diwali

Hindu and Sikh people celebrate Diwali all around the world. Diwali is called the Festival of Lights. People light special **lanterns** to celebrate Diwali.

People celebrate Diwali in different ways. Some people make pictures on their doorsteps. Some people give gifts. Some people dance together and play music.

Hanukkah

menorah

Jewish people celebrate Hanukkah all around the world. Hanukkah lasts for eight nights. People light special candles in a **menorah** to celebrate Hanukkah.

dreidel

People celebrate Hanukkah in different ways. Some people give gifts each day. Some people say prayers each night. Some people eat special foods. Some people play games with **dreidels**.

Ramadan and Id-ul-Fitr

Muslim people celebrate the month of Ramadan all around the world. During Ramadan, Muslims **fast** from sunrise to sunset. In the evening, families gather to break, or end, the fast together.

At the end of Ramadan, Muslim people celebrate Id-ul-Fitr. People eat special meals together. Many people give food to the poor.

Christmas

Christmas celebrates the birth of Jesus Christ. Christmas Day is on the 25th of December. Christian people celebrate Christmas all around the world.

Some people give gifts for Christmas. Some people go to church on Christmas. Some people sing special Christmas songs, called **carols**. Some people share a special Christmas meal.

Halloween

pumpkin

People celebrate Halloween all around the world. Halloween is on the 31st of October. Some people wear costumes. Some people carve pumpkins. Some people eat special treats.

Thanksgiving

Americans celebrate Thanksgiving. On Thanksgiving, people remember to be thankful for what they have. Some people eat a special meal on Thanksgiving.

How Do You Celebrate?

Which is your favorite holiday? How do you like to celebrate it?

Words to Know

calendar system used to measure the days and months in a year

carols special songs that people sing at Christmas to celebrate the birth of Jesus Christ

dreidel small spinning top that is used in a special game for Hanukkah

fast time when people do not eat. Many people fast for short times as part of their religion.

fireworks special objects that explode for entertainment. During a fireworks show, many fireworks are set off high in the sky.

lantern special container for a light or candle

menorah candleholder that holds nine candles. Menorahs are used during the Jewish holiday Hanukkah.

parade when people walk together down a street to celebrate an event. Often they wear special clothes.

religion system of beliefs or ideas that people live by

Index

Notes for Parents and Teachers

Before reading

Show the children the front cover of the book. Guide children in a discussion about what they think the book will be about. Can they think of a time they have been to a festival or holiday celebration? Then discuss how people all around the world celebrate holidays and festivals in different ways.

After reading

- Ask the children to think about their favorite holiday or festival. Then ask them to write about their memory explaining why it is their favorite holiday or festival. Encourage them to draw a descriptive picture to go with their writing.